JESUS' WAYS

Jesus' Ways
Copyright © 2018 by Henry L Singletary. All rights reserved

No part of this publication may be reproduced, stored in a retrieval system or transmitted in any way by any means – electronic, mechanical, photocopy, recording, or otherwise – without the prior permission of the author, except as provided by the USA copyright law.

This book is designed to provide accurate and authoritative information with regard to the subject matter covered. This information is given with the understanding that neither the author, nor Singletary Productions, LLC is engaged in rendering legal, professional advice.

Since the details of your situation are fact dependent, you should additionally seek the services of a competent professional.

Published by Singletary Productions LLC

Book design Copyright © 2017 by Singletary Productions LLC. All rights reserved.

Front cover photograph by Emma Singletary Battle
Back cover photograph by David Cooper

Published in the United States of America

ISBN: 978-0-692-99915-8

Poetry/Subjects &Themes/Inspirational & Motivational

JESUS' WAYS

Dedicated to

- *Joseph Singletary my farther you were an excellent provider .You supported me in everything I did I could always count on you. Your life showed that   The ultimate measure of a man lies not during the times of comfort and convenience, but during the times OF changelings if you can't run walk if you cant,t walk crawl but by all means keep moving. Dr. Martin Luther King Jr.*

- *Harmon Cooper Sr. My grand farther you taught me the value of hard work showed me the rewards of business ownership. I,m a better man today because of you.*

- *Willie James Cooper my uncle your words of instruction and wisdom will never be forgotten.*

- *Rufus Singletary my uncle you taught me that rewards come to those that do things the right way.*

- *John David Singletary my uncle your spirit of love and unity still lives on today.*

- *Harmon Cooper Jr. my uncle you instilled in me the need to develop a business .*

- *Jospeh Sonny Cooper my uncle you set the tone for success in business You created a very successful law practice and real estate firm. You showed us all what could be done. You passed on the secrets to all of us We thank you for that.*

- *James "Buster" Cooper my uncle you taught me that I am my brothers and sisters keeper. You were there for us at all times. We love and thank you for all that you done.*

- *Sarah Cooper Singletary my mother are that woman that the book of proverbs talks about*

JESUS' WAYS

- " Blessed is the man that finds a virtuous woman oh blessed is that man every thing she touches turns to gold you will not cause him any harm or bring him any shame at no times. When the good man leaves and goes away for a journey and comes back everything is in much better shape then it was before oh blessed is that man . You stood by our farther at all times you cared for him when he could not care for him self. You cared for him night and day with out a complaint . You are that virtuous woman
- You will be blessed and live a long life
- and you,ll remain strong . You are my best friend you constantly instill me with wisdom.
- Melvin "Robby" Cooper my uncle you taught us to " always have a dream and make sure it beams and never alow it to waste away in a stream .
- Sam Cooper my uncle you given me direction you showed me that love Has no boundaries
- David "Jr." Cooper my uncle You set the standard for all of us. You great provider farther community leader and role model. You taught and showed me how to be a business man.
- I am where I am today because of you. I,m blessed I didn,t have to look outside in the world to copy someone. You are my role model . I admire you and love you. I always wanted to be just like you. Dress
- Like you drive the same type of cars and be like you. I couldn,t have picked a better role model. After I graduated from college you talk to me and instructed me as I were your son . Congradulations of being inducted into the North Carolina Real Estate Hall of Fame Job well done.

About me, the author

I am a minister, poet, philosopher and motivational speaker who accepted the Lord when I was 9 years old. I got called to preach when I was 16, and have embraced my calling. I read the word of God daily and fast every week. I have a passion for helping people discover God's purpose for their life, and look forward to spreading God's Word through books and speaking. I give thanks and all glory to my Lord and Savior Jesus Christ for the vision and inspiration to write this book.

I am blessed with an entrepreneurial spirit and president of Singletary Productions, which is a provider of inspirational and motivational books, cards, posters and t-shirts. I also own Triangle Maintenance & Janitorial Service, a company that provides commercial and industrial janitorial services throughout the United States. When I am not working or writing, I enjoy playing golf, tennis, fishing and spending time at the beach. I am a graduate of North Carolina Agricultural & Technical State University and a veteran who served four years in the United States Marine Corps.

Contact me for speaking engagements:
SingletaryProductions@gmail.com   (336) 287-1710

JESUS' WAYS

Note from the author

I truly hope this book inspires everyone that reads it. God is truly real and his mercy endures forever. Remember what ever problem or situation you are confronted with

God will bring you through.

The lord stills makes house calls. Miracles and blessings are still given to us by god. Remember seek ye first the kingdom of god and his righteousness and all things shall be added onto it.

God bless you all

For truly the Lord is our shepherd we shall not want. We can do all things through Christ that strengthens us .we cannot live this life successfully without having a positive relationship with jesus. Success from the view of most people would be a large home , with lots of money in the bank , very educated and nice cars. All of theses things are useless without Christ. Having a relationship with jesus allows us to put things in there proper perspective. For a house is only a means of shelter, it keeps us warm from the cold and protects us from the sun. A car is merely a means of transportation. Money allows us to purchase goods and services. Education enables us to get good jobs and start successful careers.

Having a relationship with jesus allow you to put things in their proper perspective.

"Thou should have no other god before me. For we should love the god with all our heart, with all our strength with all our mind, might soul and all of our being. And we should love our neighbor as our selves. When we implement these principles in our life daily we truly will have "Jesus Ways"

JESUS' WAYS

Note to the Nation

Today our nation is going through a transition. Some of this change is good and some of it not so good. America is the leader of the free world. The world takes its guidance from us and right now we don't look so good. America, we are better than this.

A spirit of hate and separation is being spread throughout this country. The types of behavior and attitudes from our leaders aren't making America great. These attitudes never have and never will make us great.

> *It's time we had a fireside chat. The ones like President Roosevelt used to have. We need to address what's going on.*
>
> *"As a man thinketh, so is he."*
>
> *None of us should ever feel like we're superior to the next person.*

The type of thinking that causes us to disrespect others and not care about the opinions and feelings of someone because their religion is different or they came from a different ethnic group, is just wrong.

> *Today in America we need to make a New Deal like President Roosevelt once said. A New Deal that consists of respect peace, love and unity. A New Deal that enables equal access to every American regardless of race, religion, or ethnic background.*

We don't need to make America great again. America is already the greatest country in the world. In America you may be poor, illiterate, or homeless, but if you have the drive and determination, you can achieve whatever you set your mind to. That's why people from other countries have risked their lives to get here.

JESUS' WAYS

America is great and what makes us great is our diversity of cultures, religions, races and ethnic groups. When we sing the song, "God bless America", God blesses America. With the blessings we've realized, it's time to become a blessing to others. Jesus teaches us in the New Testament that we should love our neighbor as we love ourselves. (Matthew 22:39) We must make the playing field level for any American participating in the process. No more "old boy network" where all the good jobs are given to friends and relatives, many of whom are not qualified to hold the positions. This kind of inequality makes America weak. Jobs and positions need to go to the people who are the most qualified and best fit regardless of race, religion, ethnicity or personal biases.

Additionally, we need to listen to others' opinions. Too many of us are quick to judge others and don't take the time to really listen to what has been said. Sadly, a lot of us have often prejudged others. This type of behavior hurts us. We must love each other. Like the Lord loves the church, we need to have compassion, understanding and respect for each other. This is what Jesus teaches us throughout the New Testament. Hate and separation is not good for America. It never has been and never will be. It is a cancer that we Americans can't continue to let spread. Unfortunately, it has been spreading from one generation to the next. Hate is not an inherited trait. Hate is taught. We teach hate to our children. We feed them poisonous pill of hate at home so that when they come in contact with someone of another race or religion they have already formed an opinion of them. Instead of teaching hate, we must teach tolerance and mutual respect. We must base our opinions of each other not on skin color, religion or ethnicity, but, as Dr. Martin Luther King Jr. said, on "content of character". Favoritism, good old boyism and nepotism only weakens companies, operations, families, relationships, and ultimately, America.

JESUS' WAYS

The new deal that we must make, won't allow police officers to gun down Americans of any race unfairly. It will require that all police officers use deadly force only as a last result.

We must respect police officers, these men and women uphold the laws that keep us free, thriving and living the lives God has planned or us. Their work matters. Their lives matter. Police officers must also respect the Americans they are charged with protecting regardless of any perceived or real differences in race, religion, ethnicity or lifestyle. We are all God's children created in His own image and must respect each other. In the New Testament, Jesus instructs us to not judge each other. (Matthew 7:1) Judging without facts or context leads to trouble. We must practice and implement the teachings of Jesus and show each other the love of Jesus at all times.

In the New Deal America we realize that we're living in the greatest country in the world and that we all matter and each of our lives has a purpose. We educate ourselves and develop a personal relationship with God so that living together, we can fulfill his purpose.

Education will break down barriers. Full employment will reduce the need for some government services, and mean less money spent by our government on government assistant programs. When we see this New Deal at work, every American will sing:

Always have a dream and make sure that it beams.
Never allow it to waste away in a stream.

Your self-will and determination will enable you to reach your destination. Remember the Holy Bible reminds us that; "You can do all things through Christ that strengthens you." (Philippians 4:13)

To keep America great and continue to be the leader of the world, we must have the courage of President Abraham Lincoln who freed the slaves.

JESUS' WAYS

To Keep America great, we must have the wisdom and unselfishness of President john F. Kennedy and do the right thing regardless of political fallout. You must do the right thing simply because it is the right thing to do.

To keep America great, we must have the insight and foresight of President Franklin D. Roosevelt. We must face whatever challenges head on and implement policies that ensure fairness for all Americans.

We owe a debt to every American who lost their life protecting and keeping America free. This debt is owed to solders, slaves and immigrants alike. In every conflict that American solders and policemen have had to deal with — 911, Afghanistan, Iraq, The Civil War, WWI, WWII etc.— diverse soldiers fought, bled and died. We owe them. How do we repay this debt? We stay engaged, we show up, we go to the polls. We vote. We must let our voices be heard. We must represent and be represented, instead of complaining about who got elected.

Finally, we must have hope in this New Deal America. The hope that President Barack Obama inspired. The hope that Dr. Martin Luther King dreamed of. The hope that all men will realize and live out our true creed, "No man is an island, but a peninsula waiting to be connected to land. "

We need each other, must respect each other, and must give each other the love that Jesus Christ gives each of us every moment of our lives. This is what keeps America great.

May God's peace and blessings surround, guide and protect you always.

JESUS' WAYS

Singletary Productions, LLC

JESUS' WAYS

Contents

Fix Me 1
Using 2
Gold 3
Phase 4
The Sun 5
Ring 6
A Note 7
Die 8
Wife 9
Stevie Wonder 10
Your Passion 11
Personal Decay 12
Freedom 13
Know It All 14
Black People 15
Your Head 16
Control 17
Pull Together 18
The Scope of God 19
You Must 20
Action 21
Journey 22
Delight 23
My Friend 24
Fame 25
Strong 26
The Right Way 27
Let the Savior In 28
Martin and Malcolm 29
Be Mine 30
Feelings 31

JESUS' WAYS

All Things Through Christ 32
Every Now and Then 33
Sorrow 34
The Right Road 35
The Lord is Strong and Mighty 36
My Wife 38
America 40
I am 42
What Matters 44
Every American 46
America 47
Greatness 48
Oh My Brother..49
Study 50
Travel..51
Jesus Is My Light..52
It's Not About This.......................................53
To God Be The Glory 55
Hanging In The Streets 56
Amazing Grace...57
No Man Is An Island....................................58
Complete 59
Think 60
Some Folks 61
The Time You Spent 62
Time..63
Being There...64
Struggle..65
The Mask of Life 67
Fruitful and Blessed 68
You Can..69
Ambition..70
Dream...71

JESUS' WAYS

JESUS' WAYS

Fix Me

Jesus, fix me
Fix my heart
So when I speak to people, I will know I am smart
This way I won't have self-defeat.

Jesus, fix me
Fix my mind
So that I will never look behind.

Jesus, fix me
Fix my arm
So that I won't be easily influenced by the world's charm.

Jesus, fix me
Fix my head
So that when Gabriel blows his horn, I too will arise
and ascend with those that were once dead.

Using

Some people feel the only way to win in a relationship
is by abusing.
They practice the tactic of using.
This type of treatment is very confusing.
So, we all must be careful of the mate we are choosing.
This type of situation is never amusing.

JESUS' WAYS

Gold

Fool's gold comes a dime a dozen;
It's here today and gone tomorrow.
But true gold lasts forever and
increases in value every day.

Phase

Not long ago I was your age…
When many of you decided to become part of the drug craze.
I chose not to engage.

Now you walk around in a daze.
You thought it was just a phase.
It isn't when your life becomes a maze.

Now it's time to put out the blaze,
Youth please take your parents' advice…It pays.

JESUS' WAYS

The Sun

We toiled long in the sun,
Yet we still have no fun.
I often wonder how long we must continue to run,
While we continue to get burnt and beat up
by the Master's sun.

JESUS' WAYS

Ring

Love is a very splendid thing,
It often causes our heart to sing.
True love makes us go out and purchase a ring;
Joy and happiness it does bring,
Love is a very special thing.

JESUS' WAYS

A Note

Here is a note,
Just for you to tote.
The contents of it are very deep,
When you read it, it will help you fall fast asleep.
The words written inside, you should always keep;
They will help the mountains in your life
not look so steep.
Be sure to remember this whenever
your problems seem real deep.

Die

Every man will die,
That's why it's important to give life a good try.
Some things will cause us to cry;
When these occurrences happen, we should never ask God why
Because eventually we all will die.

JESUS' WAYS

Wife

I want to be your friend and man for life,
I hope one day to make you my wife.

It will be such a blessing to have you in my life;
I promise to love, protect and cherish you, and
never cause you any strife.

I want you to be more than my lover,
I want you to be my wife.

I want to be your husband and your very best friend;
Being together the two of us can win.

The rest of my life with you is what I want to spend.
I promise to stay by your side, no matter what happens,
to the very end.

I want to be your friend and man for life,
Can't you see that I love you? I'm asking you to be my wife.

It will be such a blessing to have you in my life,
So baby please, will you be my wife?

JESUS' WAYS

Stevie Wonder

Stevie you blessed us with music to hear,
It makes us stand up and cheer.

Your music teaches us how to love and conquer fear
Through the lyrics that we hear.

Thank you Stevie for making everything so clear.

JESUS' WAYS

Your Passion

You are quite a lady of fashion,
One with plenty of passion.

I can tell by your actions
You would fill me with complete satisfaction.

JESUS' WAYS

Personal Decay

It's not what you say, but how you say what you say
That often rubs people the wrong type of way.
Being sensitive really does pay.

JESUS' WAYS

Freedom

Life is the most precious thing on earth,
Next to that is freedom.
Life without freedom can become lifeless.

JESUS' WAYS

Know It All

The day that a man thinks that he knows it all,
Is the very thing that will ultimately cause him to fall.

JESUS' WAYS

Black People

Black people, Black people — we must stand tall like a church steeple,

Or we will become creeple and remain very small little people.

JESUS' WAYS

Your Head

Go to college to acquire some knowledge.
Don't go to bed without knowledge in your head
Or you may find yourself living a life of dread.

You can become tired, hungry, homeless, and
lacking enough money to buy even a loaf of bread.

If you refuse to listen, learn and read,
You may find yourself in need.
Lamenting that if only you had read,
You would not have to deal with living life very, very scared.

JESUS' WAYS

Control

Always be in control of your destiny;
Never allow anything to control you.
Always be the driver — never the passenger.

Pull Together

When we all pull together on the same spool of thread,
Then each and every one of us will be able to
buy some bread.

That way all of us can be fed
And we can stop all God's children from becoming dead;
If we just instill this one little idea into our head.

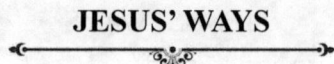

JESUS' WAYS

The Scope of God

God's horoscope gives us hope so we can cope,
Any other scope is similar to dope.
It can cause you to fall off a slope,
If you're not careful it may leave you
hanging from a rope.

JESUS' WAYS

You Must

You must
Or you will rust or turn into crust
That will form onto a bust
That will only sit idle and collect dust…
So you must.

JESUS' WAYS

Action

Talking and thinking isn't worth anything
until put into action.
That's the only way you can achieve results.

JESUS' WAYS

Journey

The hardest part of any journey is the first mile.
After that, it's just another trip.

JESUS' WAYS

Delight

You're quite a delightful sight on this or any night.
When you first came into my sight, I instantly
wanted to hold you so tight.
I knew you would fit in my arms just right.

Every time I look into your beautiful eyes,
I see such a lovely sight.
I do want to love you, but more than
just for one night.

There's no need to worry because whatever you and I
may do, I can assure you all will work out right.
Perhaps the two of us will allow our love to take flight;
From this moment forward whenever I think about you,
you will always bring delight.

My Friend

Thank you Jesus for being my friend.
You freed me from all my sins.
Because of You I don't let problems get next to my skin.
So glad I decided to let You in,
You've always been my one and true friend;
Someone to stick by my side not only now,
But to the very end.

JESUS' WAYS

Fame

Fame without Christ can cause you a lot of shame;
If you're not careful, you can end up being
burned by Satan's flame.

You get caught up and look to point your finger at someone,
But it's yourself where you need to place the blame.

Life is serious and real — it's more than just a game…
The Lord left us the knowledge and wisdom
in the bible when He came.

JESUS' WAYS

Strong

God will keep you strong.
Only He can keep us from doing wrong….
Let Him place inside you a new song.

Jesus is so real,
He knows all about us and how we feel.
Let Him take you by the hand,
With Him you will always be able to stand.

Don't you know it was He not one of us who created man?

God will keep you strong.
Following Him will enable you to live a life
filled with blessings…
A life that will be very long.

God's Holy Spirit will give you a new song.
He is ready to show you the way…
Why don't you choose Him today?

Time won't just sit still;
Your life is what Satan wants to steal.
He's out to destroy, corrupt, mislead you and kill.
God will never mislead or disappoint us;
In Him is where we need to always trust.

God will keep you strong.

JESUS' WAYS

The Right Way

Lord, I owe you my entire life.
You took me away from a world filled with strife.
Thank you Lord for being so good,
Only You could do the things that no man could.

Your promises You always keep;
Even when things in my life seem so steep.
I often times lose my way;
I need you Lord.... right now and everyday.

Because of You I have real peace,
It's good to know that Your righteousness will never cease.
I need you Lord to guide my way,
Teach me daily how to pray.

Let the Savior In

Let the Savior in
God will show you how to win.

You don't have to die
Just give God a try.

He knows how you feel
God is so for real.

Let Jesus be your friend —
He'll take away your sins.

I'm talking to my brother and my sisters too,
Our days are numbered and are so few.

Call on His name,
You'll never be the same.
He'll take away all of your pain,

Oh yes He will,
He knows how you feel.
It is getting late.
And time just won't sit still,
We all need to know and do Jesus' will.

JESUS' WAYS

Martin and Malcolm

Malcolm didn't die for nothing;
Let's not turn Martin's life into shame.
It's not the system but ourselves where we must
place some of the blame.

While they were living they gave us the right seed,
Yet too many people live a life filled with greed.

They planted their flowers,
Many didn't flourish,
Some turned into weeds.

Malcolm didn't die for nothing;
Let's not turn Martin's life into shame.

Since they both have left us,
this world just hasn't been the same.
They gave us instruction and showed us
how to play life's game,
I'm sick and tired of watching people destroy themselves
selling and abusing cocaine.

This type of living causes one's life to become insane.
Righteous knowledge is what we all must
put inside our brains.

Malcolm didn't die for nothing;
Let's not turn Martin's life into shame.

Too many of our people's lives have become filled with pain.
We need to hitch a ride and take a seat on Jesus' train.

JESUS' WAYS

Be Mine

I can't get you off my mind
Please don't go away…
With me is where you need to stay.

I know you've been hurt before;
Please don't use me and leave me here in
an attempt to even the score.

You're the girl I have been asking the Lord for.
I'm going to love you more and more.

Baby I want you to be mine,
I can't get you out of my mind.

I want to hold you tight…
More than just for one night.

You look so good to me;
When I kissed your lips I was set free.

I want to make you mine —
Baby you are so fine.

I want to be your man.
If you let me I know I can.

Baby I know how you feel….
My love for you is real.

Baby please don't run away,
With me is where you need to stay.

JESUS' WAYS

Feelings

I don't want your feelings to ever go away;
With you is where I want to stay.

I'm so tired of being alone.
I'm waiting patiently — hoping you will phone.

You're the only girl for me,
The touch of your lips sets my cold heart free.
You have all my love and all my heart — here is the key.

I love you too much,
Baby please let me feel your touch.

I just want to feel you over and over again;
Please tell me this is the beginning and not the end.
Time with you is what I want to spend.

JESUS' WAYS

All Things Through Christ

I can do all things through Christ Who strengthens me.

I was living life blind and couldn't see,
I prayed to the Lord and He set me free.

Every one of us at times gets confused
And nobody likes being used.

Call on Jesus and He'll show you the way;
He will surely make everything okay.

JESUS' WAYS

Every Now and Then

I know sometimes that this old world gets you down
And when you need a friend not a one can be found.
But when you let Jesus in, He'll turn your whole life around.

When your work is done, you will be assured
to receive a crown.
That way you'll know for sure, your soul
will be heaven bound.

Sometimes in life we all do things that are just not smart.
Call on Jesus and He'll give you a brand new start.

One thing about Him is that it doesn't matter
the color of your skin,
Jesus Christ will free us from our sins.
Everywhere I go I see so many people decaying;
That's why we need to do what the preacher has been saying.

JESUS' WAYS

Sorrow

We must develop our future leaders of tomorrow
Or we are destined to be a community that
will always borrow.

That reality will fill us with so much sorrow,
Because we'll fear there may never be a tomorrow.

Especially with this current drug horror
That's causing America so much sorrow.

JESUS' WAYS

The Right Road

The right road is a long road,
which often requires us to carry a heavy load
To places of treasures and gold.

The wrong road appears to be a shorter road
Where some don't even carry a load.
Yet at any time their life can unfold,
Leaving them out in the cold.

JESUS' WAYS

The Lord is Strong and Mighty

JESUS' WAYS

The Lord is strong, mighty and full of grace,
I'm looking forward to one day seeing His face.

All praise and glory to His name,
I thank Him for taking away all my sins and shame.

I'm only seeking God's blessing and peace,
not glory and fame,
Living my life without Him will only cause pain.

We all need to realize and understand
the real reason the Lord came,
When you allow Him to enter your life,
you will never be the same.

JESUS' WAYS

My Wife

I'm seeking someone who will become my best friend,
companion and wife;
Someone I will always cherish, honor and love
throughout my life.
Someone I will enhance and never cause any strife.
Someone I will respect and always love,
Whom I will only place God above.

Someone I will never make cry,
Someone I will always kiss and wipe any tears dry,
Someone willing and ready to give love a try.

For her I'll gladly shed a tear,
I will be so happy whenever she is near.

I will live to love and keep her near,
I will always show her love, compassion and understanding
and never cause her to fear.

So darling, why don't you come to me
right now — I'm here.
I will always love and cherish you and fill you with cheer.

JESUS' WAYS

America

America was formed on the principles of freedom of speech and freedom of religion. God created man and woman in his own image and everything God created was good.

We are a country made up of different races, religions and cultures. This makes us unique. We are Black Americans, Asian Americans, White Americans, Native Americans, Jewish Americans, Catholic Americans and more. America is a melting pot of different ethnicities. This makes us special.

While we don't always agree with each other, we must love and respect each other. Jesus instructs us to love our neighbors as we do ourselves.

JESUS' WAYS

JESUS' WAYS

I am

I am who I am.
I am what I am.

You must either accept me for who I am
or respect me for what I am.
I am sorry that I can't be who you want me to be.
If I were to be any other way, I wouldn't be me.

JESUS' WAYS

JESUS' WAYS

What Matters

We may not like what someone says or does,
but we must respect each other.
It's not just about Black Lives Matter, White
Lives Matter, or Blue Lives Matter,

All Lives Matter.

All of us desire and want the same things…nice housing,
great jobs, good education, affordable healthcare,
safe neighborhoods, fair treatment, and equal access
to all that America has to offer.

JESUS' WAYS

JESUS' WAYS

Every American

Our constitution gives every American the right to free speech and pursuit of happiness.

The Bill of Rights and passage of Civil Rights laws provides for every American to have access to opportunities regardless of race, religion or ethnic background.

JESUS' WAYS

America

If America is to be great,
We must realize that it's getting late.
How long do we expect Jesus to wait?
We can't continue to eat food from Satan's plate.
That food will only continue to fill us with hate.
We need to stop and accept Jesus Christ as our mate.
Because sooner or later we'll meet Jesus on our chosen date.
It is Jesus who can cleanse our sinful slate.
And, Jesus can change America's state.
Andy really make America great.

Greatness

What will make America great is living out the ideals of our constitution, the Bill of Rights, the Civil Rights Act, and the ideals of our founding fathers.

Honoring the legacies of Dr. Martin Luther King, President John F. Kennedy, and President Barack Obama will keep America Great.

JESUS' WAYS

Oh My Brother

There was a time we used to help each other out
Now when someone offers us a hand
we are filled with doubt.
Oh my brother we need to show more love
towards one another.
I'm tired of seeing people down
it's time we brought them around
They don't have to eat food of the ground.
No one seems to really care
It's time for all of us to share.

Oh my brother we need to show more love
towards one another.
It's time to understand that God created
the world for all men.
These people don't have to sleep on the street
why don't you help the next person you meet.

Dot every I and cross every T
I haven't dotted every I and crossed every T

Jesus is the only hope for folks like you and me
Only he can set us free.

JESUS' WAYS

Study

Man if you read and study my word
I can assure you tat you will be able to pass any test.

Because of me King David was able to conquer his quest.

When you have company please don't forget to
introduce me as your friend to all of your guests.

When you lie down at night I'll give you peaceful rest
I'll make sure you always be at your best.

It was I who put Adam to sleep and took a piece
of rib out of Eve's breast

Follow me and wherever you go in your life
you will have the best.

JESUS' WAYS

Travel

Being alone is sometimes the best way to travel
especially when things around you begin to unravel.

People you thought you could trust will often
turn the truth into gravel.

That's why it's best sometimes to be alone when you travel.

JESUS' WAYS

Jesus Is My Light

Jesus is my light that gives me so much sight
When I allowed him to hold me tight.
He turned all my sins from red to white
He's the reason why my soul feels so right.
Through him I know I will win the fight
for he enables me to do what's right.

JESUS' WAYS

It's Not About This

It's not about this
It's not about that
It's not about the friendly pats on the back.

It's about being real
Only God can show you how to deal.

It's about being good
Doing the things that you should.

It's not about this
It's not about that
It's not about eating all you can and getting fat.

It's not about this
It's not about that
It's about living good
Trying to do the things you know you should.

It's getting late
How long do you think the king is going to wait.
Better clean your slate.

It's not about this
It's not about that
It's not about the friendly pats on the back.

It's about being real
Letting people know how you feel.
You can't make it on your own
The world will tease you and leave you all alone.
Before you know it you will be gone.

JESUS' WAYS

It's not about this
It's not about that
It's not about the friendly pats on the back.
It's about trying to start educating people about power
and love of Jesus and dangers of marijuana, heroin,
prescription drugs and crack.

It's not about this
It's not about that.

To God Be The Glory

To God be the glory
Lord help me tell your story.
The day I left you my life started to decay
Jesus I need your help throughout the day.
I thought I was so tough
Living without you only made my life rough.

To God be the glory
Lord use me I'll tell the story.

Your word is so right
It allowed me to see the light.

Lord I just want to praise you
You are always so true.

God you deserve all the glory
Yes I'll tell your story.
My life had become full of sin
I was living on the edge heading for the end.

To God be the glory
Use me I'll tell the story.

Hanging In The Streets

Always feeling like you got to get out
So you go hang in the street.
Going to show the world you got clout
Don't be surprised who you might meet.
Everything you see ain't sweet.

Never want to stay at home
Leaving your sweet lady all alone.
Hanging in the streets.

Never really know what you will meet
Never take the time to take your baby out.
This only makes her sit at home and pout
Hanging in the streets.

Some of the ladies out there do look really sweet
Don't you know your love at home can't be beat.

Wake up my friend and see the light
Go home and love that woman right.
Never gonna find another one that will love you so sweet
The lady at home is the real treat.

JESUS' WAYS

Amazing Grace

Amazing grace how sweet the sound.
People don't you worry when they place me in the ground,
I'll just lie that there and wait until Gabriel's trumpet sounds.

Amazing grace I have run my race
Now I'm looking forward to seeing Jesus face.
Don't you know God has prepared me for a better place.

Amazing grace how sweet the sound.
Peace joy and happiness in him is what I found,
Don't fret too much for me, my soul is heaven bound.

Amazing grace how sweet the sound.
People we all need to get it together,
God is continuing to make his rounds.

JESUS' WAYS

No Man is a Island

No man is a Island,
but a peninsula waiting to be connected to land.

JESUS' WAYS

Complete

We must take the best from each of us.
That will complete all of us.

JESUS' WAYS

Think

As a man thinketh so is he.

JESUS' WAYS

Some Folks

Some folks need to understand that it's God
not you who own this land.
Some folks need to understand it's God
not you who created man.

Just the other the day I heard about
some innocent folks that were killed.
Many of them were so young
I'm sure they left us with out a will.

White ones, Black ones, Brown ones,
Red ones and Yellow ones.
Instead of giving us hope you only fill us up
with doubt.
But you expect God's children to walk around
with their head held down
Walking around with a pout, but the holy ghost of God
inside them make them stand tall
And praise the Lord and shout.

But some folks need to understand it's God
not you created man.
But some folks need to understand it's God
not you who holds my hand.

Some folks just need to understand.

JESUS' WAYS

The Time You Spent

Thank you Jesus for the time you spent
How can we ever repay you for our life's rent.

You came preaching salvation,
offering it free wherever you went.

Yet many of your own folk, were filled with
so much resentment
Not knowing in fact you were God in the flesh who was sent.

Thank you Jesus for the time that you spent.

JESUS' WAYS

Time

Time has been a friend of mine
For I didn't allow it to unwind and become twine.

I learned very early that it would not last
And it moved very constantly and fast
Yet I was prepared to meet fate's blast
For I knew I too would become just a memory of the past.

How ever you must remember, I am not the
first nor last who's time will surely pass.

Being There

Thank you Jesus for being there
You are always able and willing to share.

Your words are so just and fair
You have answered my prayer
For your presence is everywhere

Thank you just for being there.

JESUS' WAYS

Struggle

I struggled so much
it feels like I lost my touch.

Yet this is not the end
I'll give life one more spin
Sooner or later I will win.

You struggle so much
Never use failure as a crutch.

Times have been hard
You can always call on God
He'll give you a brand new start.

So don't get down
His presence is all around.

Life is a gamble
Some things we do become shambles
But that doesn't mean we should stop
Keep trying to you reach the top

You struggle so much
Never use failure as a crutch.

Get up and try once again
Sooner or later you will win

We all struggle a lot
Hoping to put gold in our pot

JESUS' WAYS

Times do get hard
Yet we can count on God
He'll give you a brand new start.

Now be your best friend
Hold up your chin
Sooner or later you will win.

When everything looks bad
Never get mad
Things will change to make your heart glad.

Some things we do aren't always smart
Remember you can count on God
He'll give you a brand new start.

JESUS' WAYS

The Mask of Life

Don't live life behind a mask
Or you subject to fall into the wrong type of cast.

We should live each day as if were our last
Because time goes by so fast
And life eventually doesn't last.

Make sure you take time to learn
things from the past
Because sooner or later we all will become
a memory of the past.

JESUS' WAYS

Fruitful and Blessed

When you allow the Lord into your life
that's the only way
You can be at your best.

Before that your life has been an awful mess
You constantly living a life filled with with stress
Everything you do seems to turn into a mess.

Satan continues to ride you and
put you through all kinds of tests.

Its time to live life on Gods words and prayer,
not speculation
And a guess.

Jesus will fill you with his holy spirit
and you will be able to
Pass all of life's tests.

With Jesus your life will instantly become successful,
fruitful and blessed.
He'll take away all of your stress.

JESUS' WAYS

You Can

You can for you are a man
Not some wind blowing from a fan.
Aren't you the man that made the fan
And does not you hand place trash in the can.

You can.

Ambition

Ambition is some of the best nutrition
As long as we don't turn our restrictions in to fiction.

JESUS' WAYS

Dream

Always have a dream
And make sure it beams
And never allow it to
waste away in a stream.

JESUS' WAYS

Copyright© 2018 by Henry L Singletary. All rights reserved

No part of this publication may be reproduced, stored in a retrieval system or transmitted in any way by any means - electronic, mechanical, photocopy, recording, or otherwise - without the prior permission of the author, except as provided by the USA copyright law.

The opinions expressed by the author are not necessarily those of Singletary Productions, LLC.

www.ingramcontent.com/pod-product-compliance
Lightning Source LLC
LaVergne TN
LVHW051510070426
835507LV00022B/3031